AMERICAN MUSEUM
OF NATURAL HISTORY

STERLING CHILDREN'S BOOKS
New York

An Imprint of Sterling Publishing
1166 Avenue of the Americas
New York, NY 10036

ISBN 978-1-4549-2701-3

Distributed in Canada by Sterling Publishing
c/o Canadian Manda Group, 664 Annette Street
Toronto, Ontario, Canada M6S 2C8
Distributed in the United Kingdom by GMC Distribution Services
Castle Place, 166 High Street, Lewes, East Sussex, England BN7 1XU
Distributed in Australia by NewSouth Books, 45 Beach Street, Coogee, NSW 2034, Australia

For information about custom editions, special sales, and premium and corporate purchases, please contact
Sterling Special Sales at 800-805-5489 or specialsales@sterlingpublishing.com.

Manufactured in China
Lot #:
2 4 6 8 10 9 7 5 3 1
10/17

sterlingpublishing.com

Text written by Ben Richmond

Photo credits: age fotostock: © SuperStock: 24; Alamy: © robertharding: 25–26, © David Tipling Photo
Library: 23, back endpaper; Arcticphoto: © Bryan and Cherry Alexander: 8; Getty Images: © Doug Allan: 7,
© Paul Nicklen/National Geographic Creative: 12; iStock: © Keith Szafranski: 11, © vladsilver: 9 left; Minden
Pictures: © Stefan Christmann/BIA: 6, 19, © Antoine Dervaux/Biosphoto: 17–18, © Klein and Hubert: front
endpaper, 13, © Fred Olivier/NPL: 9 right, © Mark Spencer/Auscape II: 21, © Winfried Wisniewski/FLPA:
27–28, © Norbert Wu: 22; NaturePL: © Klein & Hubert: front & back cover, 4, © Pete Oxford: 20; Photoshot:
© T. Milse @wildllife/NHPA: 16; SuperStock: © Fritz Poelking: 14, © M. Watson/ardea.com: 10

Capitalization of bird names in this book reflects common style and not
that of the ornithological community.

AMERICAN MUSEUM ᴏꜰ NATURAL HISTORY

Baby Penguin's First Waddles

STERLING CHILDREN'S BOOKS
New York

It is fall in Antarctica when a female emperor penguin lays her egg. The temperature in Antarctica is below freezing, yet emperor penguins are able to live here year round. Emperor penguins are the largest species of penguin. On average, they are about four feet tall and weigh nearly 50 pounds.

After the female penguin has laid her egg, she travels to the ocean to find food. Her male partner stays behind to care for the egg.

The male penguin balances the egg on his toes and tucks the egg under a feathered flap of skin to keep it warm. He waits and waits for his partner to return.

After about two months, the female returns with a belly full of food—and the baby penguin hatches! The male has not eaten in months. He can finally travel to the ocean and have a meal.

Baby penguins are called chicks. Chicks are the youngest members of the penguin colony.

The chick waddles around in the snow. The world is a big place. There is much to explore!

The chick's mother has food in her belly. She regurgitates, or throws up, this food into her chick's mouth. The chick will depend on her parents for food for another five months. Until then, the mother and father will take turns caring for the chick and finding food.

Emperor penguins eat fish, krill, and squid. They use their long beaks to snatch up prey, and they swallow their food whole, without chewing.

After two months, the chick starts to become more independent. She still needs her parents for food, but she spends more time with other chicks.

This group of chicks is called a crèche. Some adult penguins try and protect the chicks from birds called southern giant petrels that are looking for an easy meal.

It's time to eat again! The parents call to their chick in a loud cry, and the chick responds with a soft whistle.

Every family has a special call that only members of the same family use. This way, parents feed only their own chick and not others.

Like the chicks, adult emperor penguins also gather in groups. They huddle together, and eventually, the penguins on the outside move to the inside where it's nice and toasty. No one is cold for too long.

By summer, the ice begins to break up, and the chick begins to fledge. This means that she is losing her baby feathers and becoming an adult penguin.

The chick begins learning how to swim and find food. Once she masters these skills, she will no longer need her parents; she will be totally independent.

The chick dives into the water. *SPLASH!* Emperor penguins are not the most graceful at walking, but they are amazing swimmers. Their sleek bodies and strong flippers help them swim fast. They can dive as deep as 1,850 feet and hold their breath for up to 20 minutes.

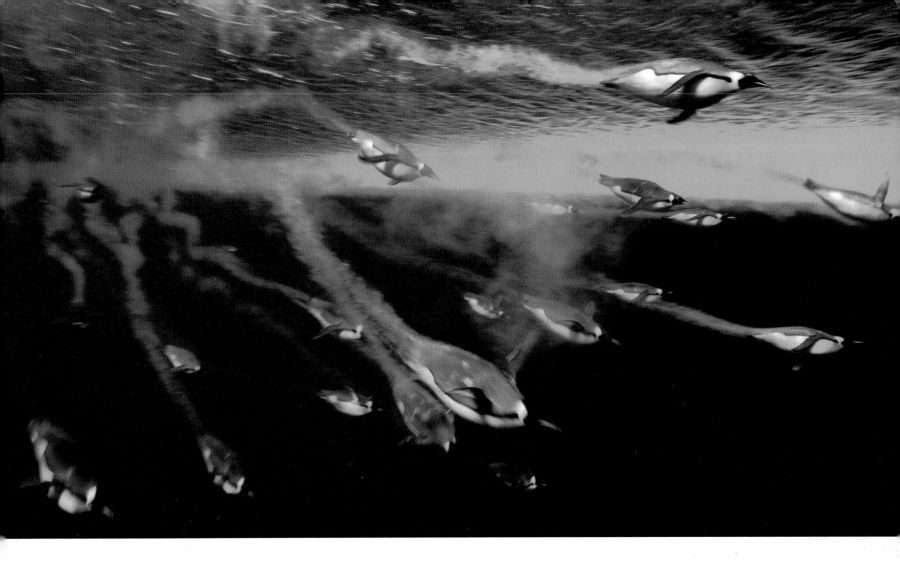

While swimming, their feathers help them blend in with the ocean. From below, a penguin's white belly blends with the light water above. From above, their dark back blends with the dark water below. This effect is called counter-shading, and it helps penguins hide from predators, like leopard seals, as well as prey.

Another way that penguins get around is by tobogganing. This is when penguins slide on their bellies, using their flippers and feet to help scoot them along when needed.

A penguin stands on top of an icy hill and slides all the way down. *Wheee!*

The chick is one year old now. She has lost all her baby feathers and is able to find food on her own. She is now perfectly suited to live in one of the harshest places on Earth.

Every year, she sheds her feathers and replaces them with a new coat. This is called molting. Molting helps keep emperor penguins warm year after year in the cold Antarctic weather.

Emperor penguins live well in the cold, but human activity is making Earth warmer. This means that these penguins' home is slowly melting. Scientists around the world are working to stop this. Emperor penguins are incredible animals, and their home is worth saving!

Meet the Expert

My name is **Paul Sweet**, and I am the Collections Manager in the Ornithology department at the American Museum of Natural History. I have been interested in natural history and birds for as long as I can remember! Before moving to New York City, I studied birds in Singapore and in my home country of England. I have worked at the American Museum of Natural History for more than 25 years. The Museum is home to the largest and most diverse collection of bird specimens in the world. Did you know that some prehistoric penguins were bigger than humans?